W9-AAV-150

WOOLLY MAMMOTHS

BY **GINGER WADSWORTH**

ILLUSTRATIONS BY **TODD ZALEWSKI**

On My Own
SCIENCE

M Millbrook Press/Minneapolis

Text copyright © 2006 by Ginger Wadsworth
Illustrations copyright © 2006 by Todd Zalewski

All rights reserved. International copyright secured. No part of this book may be
reproduced, stored in a retrieval system, or transmitted in any form or by any means—
electronic, mechanical, photocopying, recording, or otherwise—without the prior
written permission of Lerner Publishing Group, except for the inclusion of brief
quotations in an acknowledged review.

Millbrook Press, Inc.
A division of Lerner Publishing Group
241 First Avenue North
Minneapolis, MN 55401 U.S.A.

Website address: www.lernerbooks.com

Library of Congress Cataloging-in-Publication Data

Wadsworth, Ginger.
    Woolly mammoths / by Ginger Wadsworth ; illustrations by Todd Zalewski.
       p.   cm. — (On my own science)
    ISBN-13: 978–1–57505–879–5 (lib. bdg. : alk. paper)
    ISBN-10: 1–57505–879–0 (lib. bdg. : alk. paper)
    1. Woolly mammoth—Juvenile literature. I. Zalewski, Todd, ill. II. Title. III. Series.
  QE882.P8W33 2006
  569'.67—dc22   2005010433

Manufactured in the United States of America
2 3 4 5 6 7 – JR – 11 10 09 08 07 06

To Collin and Justin,
who already love to dig in the dirt
—G.W.

Modern Times

It is hot and dry in California's desert.
Under a tent, scientists dig in the sand.
They are looking for mammoths,
giant elephant-like creatures.
But the scientists are not looking for
living mammoths.
Mammoths died out about 4,000 years ago.
These scientists are paleontologists.
They study past life on Earth.
They learn by looking at fossils, the
hardened tracks or remains of animals.
Paleontologists have studied fossils of
mammoths found all over the world.

Scientists know that Earth was different
when mammoths lived.
Thousands of years ago, this part of
California was a lake, not a desert.
Mammoths came to eat the grass
that grew around the lake.
Some of them died here.
Over time, mud and sand buried the bones.

Scientists have found about 100 mammoth fossils in California's desert.

Most are small parts of bones and teeth.

They have also found fossils of bathtub-sized tortoises and giant bears.

Like mammoths, these animals are extinct.

None are still living.

But what caused the mammoths to die out?

Scientists are looking for the answer
here in the desert.
A scientist has spotted a piece of bone.
She yells out, and everyone comes to help.
They brush away the earth with tiny tools.
They sift the sand through a screen.
Soon they uncover the fossil.
It's part of a baby mammoth's skull!
The skull will be studied at a museum.
Scientists want to know how this baby died.
The answers may not explain how
mammoths became extinct.
But every bit of information helps scientists
complete the mammoth story.

Mammoth Parts

Mammoths lived on Earth for more than
three million years.
They looked much like modern elephants.
They had the same body shape and long trunk.
They walked on four sturdy legs.
But mammoths were not elephants.
Mammoth bones were thicker and heavier.

Mammoths lived in Europe, Asia, and North America.

One type of mammoth, the Columbian mammoth, weighed 9 to 11 tons.

That is about as much as 130 adult people.

The steppe mammoth was even heavier.

It was the largest mammoth that ever lived.

Adult steppe mammoths
stood taller than 14 feet.
Male woolly mammoths weighed 4 to 6 tons.
That's about what six cars weigh.
They stood 9 to 11 feet tall at the shoulder.
Each foot was as big as a dinner plate.
Females, called cows, were smaller.

All mammoths had two curved tusks.

Tusks are long teeth.

But unlike our teeth, mammoth
tusks grew 1 to 6 inches each year.
Stretched out straight, some mammoth tusks
would have been longer than a bed.

14

Paleontologists have found tusks
with chips and breaks.
From these markings, scientists learn how
mammoths used their tusks.
They worked like a forklift to move objects.
Bulls used them to fight other males.
And mammoths shook their tusks to scare
away enemies, such as saber-toothed cats.

Mammoths could use their tusks to
chop holes in the ice and get water.
Mammoths sucked up more than
2 gallons of water into their trunks.
Then they squirted the water into their
mouths, just like elephants do.
At the tip of a mammoth's trunk
was its nose.
A mammoth's trunk was about 6 feet long.
Its trunk has many muscles, but no bones.
The trunk could move in every direction.
By pushing air out of their trunks,
mammoths could make sounds.

Adult mammoths had four teeth.

Each tooth was as large as a big brick
and weighed about 4 pounds.

Mammoths ate about 300 pounds of
tough grasses every day.

All that chewing wore down their teeth.

Their teeth fell out one by one.

But a new set moved into place.

Each mammoth had six sets of teeth.

When old mammoths lost their last
set of teeth, they could not eat.

They died of hunger.

Some of their bodies turned into fossils.

Scientists find the fossils and study them.

Mammoths Change

From studying fossils, scientists can tell
when a mammoth lived and
what type of mammoth it was.
Early mammoths are called *Mammuthus
meridionalis*.
This type lived for two million years.

These early mammoths traveled across
Europe and Asia.
Some went north to the Arctic Circle.
Others reached North America.
Warm tropical forests covered much of
the world's land.

Very slowly, Earth's weather changed.
About two million years ago,
Earth became cooler.
It was the start of the Ice Age.
In some places, the snow never melted.
Thick sheets of ice called glaciers covered
the northern parts of Earth.
Nearly half of Earth was covered with ice.
Animals had to change to survive.

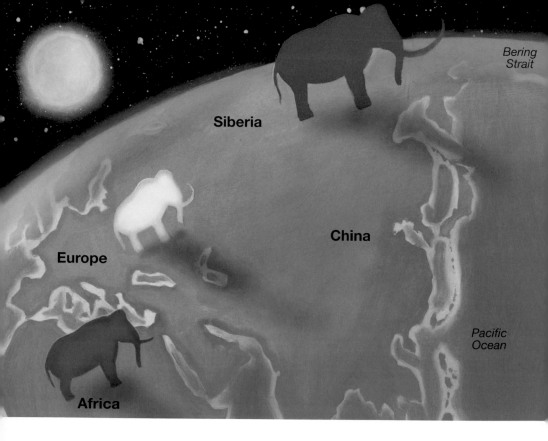

Mammuthus meridionalis changed slowly.
Earth changed faster than it could.
Mammuthus meridionalis couldn't live
in the colder weather, so it died out.
Newer types of mammoths handled
Earth's changing weather better than
Mammuthus meridionalis did.

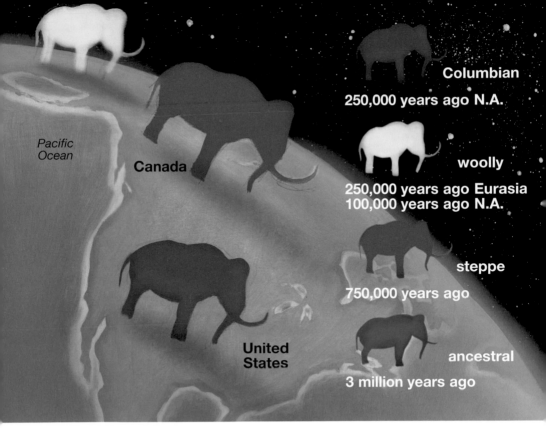

Pacific Ocean

Canada

Columbian
250,000 years ago N.A.

woolly
250,000 years ago Eurasia
100,000 years ago N.A.

steppe
750,000 years ago

United States

ancestral
3 million years ago

The Columbian mammoth roamed
North America, eating grass and plants.
It migrated as far south as Mexico.
The steppe mammoth lived in the wide-open
spaces of Europe and Asia.
But as Earth cooled more, they died too.
Only the woolly mammoth was left!

The woolly mammoth's body was
perfect for the Ice Age.
Thick skin and fat kept woolly
mammoths warm.
A hump above their shoulders stored fat.
The fat gave woolly mammoths energy
if they could not find enough food to eat.

Fur covered mammoths from head to toe.

Even their trunks had fur.

An underlayer of soft wool kept woolly mammoths even warmer.

Scientists know this from their discoveries.

In Russian Siberia and other places, the ground stays frozen all year long.

In these places, scientists have found frozen mammoths thousands of years old.

Their fur was black or brown.

Scientists were also able to look inside a mammoth's stomach.

They found grass.

This find told them what mammoths ate.

Each clue helped scientists understand mammoths better.

Life in the Herd
300,000–500,000 years ago

Large groups of woolly mammoths roamed
the lands of Europe and Asia.
This northern part of Earth stayed
shivery cold.
The ocean froze near the Bering Strait
between Asia and North America.
It made a perfect bridge.
Scientists think that is how woolly
mammoths walked to North America.

Like other mammoths, woolly mammoths
lived in groups called herds.
A herd was made up of female mammoths
and their young.
The oldest cow was usually the leader.
She may have been 60 years old or more.
Bulls probably lived with other males.
Scientists believe this from watching
modern-day elephants.

Herds of mammoths were often
on the move, searching for food.
Mammoths ate and looked for food
alongside other plant eaters.
There were herds of ancient types of
caribou, bison, and giant elk.
Sometimes, there was not enough food.
Perhaps a shortage of food caused all
of these animals to become extinct.

A baby mammoth grew inside its mother
for 22 months.

Once born, mammoth babies had to be
protected from predators.

There were meat-eating wolves and bears
waiting for a calf to wander away.

Saber-toothed cats attacked with sharp teeth.

Adult mammoths risked their lives
to guard the calves.
Scientists believe this from watching
modern elephants.
Scientists wonder if mammoths
died out because more mammoths
were killed each year than were born.

People and Woolly Mammoths

Early people began to share the land
with woolly mammoths.
People hunted mammoths for their meat.
Mammoth fur and skin helped people
stay warm.
People carved tools and weapons
from the bones.
Hunting mammoths was a difficult task.
Early people had to figure out
how to trap mammoths.
Scientists have put together ideas of
how people hunted mammoths.

Hunters probably crept close to herds of
mammoths and hid.
Then the hunters jumped up and
waved blazing torches at the mammoths.
The adults would have circled the babies.
But the hunters threw sharp, stone-tipped
spears at the mammoths.

The spears could pierce a mammoth's heart.
The hunters took meat and bones
from the dead mammoths.
They left the rest and headed home.
But could early people have killed off all
the mammoths?
Scientists aren't sure.

Scientists do know that about 10,000 years ago, Earth became much warmer.

The Ice Age was ending.

Forests began to grow in the south.

New plants replaced the grasses.

Western North America turned into a desert.

Without good grass, the mammoths could not survive.

There were fewer and fewer mammoths.

And then there were none.

What killed off the mammoths?
Paleontologists search for clues.
They dig through the dirt to find
mammoth fossils and bones.
They look at the pictures that early
people drew inside their caves.
The cave pictures tell many stories.
They show family life, mammoth hunts,
and other animals from long ago.
Yet most of those animals are gone.
Did human hunters kill all the mammoths?
Did the change in the weather kill them?
Or did mammoths die from a sickness?
Maybe something else happened.

Finding the answers is like working
on a puzzle.
Some of the pieces don't seem to fit.
Other pieces are still missing.
Maybe you will grow up to be a
paleontologist.
You can help finish the puzzle
and solve the mystery.
Why are mammoths extinct?